working with precut

Precuts are wonderful. As you can see from my patterns, I love to work with them. They are color coordinated, so there is no more roaming around the quilt shop for hours trying to pick out fabric that matches just right. They are economical because, basically, you are buying just enough for your project. As an added bonus, they save time with cutting because a lot of the work has already been done for you!

Not every precut bundle is right for every pattern. Please take care in reading the pattern to see how many strips or squares you'll need that will contrast with the white or cream fabric in the project. (Basically, if there is white in the pattern, all of the strips need to contrast.) Keep in mind, even a busy print on a white or cream background can have good contrast. Most of the patterns don't require you to use all of the precut fabrics, so feel free to set aside some for another project.

Also remember that you can choose whatever neutral fabric you prefer, such as gray or black, or any color that contrasts with the majority of the colors in your chosen precut bundle. I love working with white or ivory because it matches everything, always looks great, and I always have some in my house. When I get inspired, I grab a Jelly Roll or Layer Cake from my closet, and then I am off and running.

For those of you unfamiliar with precut fabrics, here is a brief rundown. Keep in mind that different companies may call their bundles by different names. Companies also put different numbers of strips and squares in their bundles, so be sure you know how many you need for your project before you buy your fabric. I usually buy bundles with 40 to 42 strips or squares, and all of those will work for the patterns in this book.

- **Jelly Rolls** are bundles of 2½"-wide strips. They contain between 20 and 40 strips.

- **Layer Cake**s are bundles of 10" squares. They contain between 20 and 42 squares. These can easily be cut into 5" squares and used in patterns that call for charm squares.

- **Charm packs** are bundles of 5" squares. A bundle contains between 20 and 42 squares.

Important Notes about Precuts

- Remember, you don't have to use precuts to make the quilts from this book. The projects are still quick and easy when you use scraps from your fabric stash.

- *Do not wash* precut fabric! It will shrink, fray, and no longer have the correct dimensions to make your quilt.

- Many people wonder how to deal with the pinked edges of the precut fabrics. When aligning your fabric for cutting and sewing, always use the outer points of the pinked edges as the edge of the fabric.

quiltmaking basics

If you're new to quilting, I strongly suggest taking a beginner class at a local quilt shop. If that is not feasible, the Internet is a great learning tool. There are endless videos posted to help you learn every aspect of quiltmaking—take advantage of them! Even if you are a beginner, you can make a great quilt. Please read through this section to learn some helpful hints I use every day in my quilting. With a little practice and a little patience, you will learn to make quilts like a pro!

Cutting and Piecing

Accurately cutting your pieces is the first step to ensuring that your segments and blocks are the correct measurements. Many people suggest stacking the strips or squares and then cutting them. The more you stack, the more inaccurate your pieces will be. I suggest starting out by stacking two layers and cutting. After you're confident your pieces are coming out accurately, you can cut additional layers. Four is the maximum number of strips or squares that I stack for cutting.

Tools Needed

I deem these tools invaluable when it comes to making a quilt. You will need all of these tools to complete the various quilts in this book:

- Rotary cutter, 45 mm or 60 mm
- Self-healing cutting mat, at least 18" × 24"
- 6" × 24" acrylic ruler
- 12½" square ruler
- 6½" square ruler (optional, but very useful)

Seam Allowances

The quilts made for this book were all sewn using a scant ¼"-wide seam allowance. This means I sew my seams *slightly* smaller than ¼" wide. The edge of my fabric brushes against the ¼" line on my sewing machine. I find that when I use a true ¼"-wide seam allowance, all of my pieced segments and blocks come out too small. At least with a scant ¼"-wide seam allowance, my block has a chance of being the right size! If your block is a bit larger than it should be, you can always trim it to the correct size, or you may want to increase your seam allowance just slightly.

Trim Those Threads

When you work with white, it's easy for loose threads to show through your finished quilt after it's quilted. To prevent this, trim all loose threads as you are sewing, *especially dark threads*.

Pressing

For all of the patterns in this book, press the seam allowances toward the darker fabric, unless otherwise noted. If you have a choice, never press toward white fabric. The darker fabric will show through your quilt top and you will regret it! If you use a dark fabric instead of white, feel free to reverse the pressing directions as you assemble the blocks and quilt top.

Where two seams meet, the seam allowances should be positioned in opposite directions. These seams will butt against each other. I always place my pins at the intersecting seams when I'm sewing longer strips together. If it's a small piece with just one intersecting seam, I hold it in place with my fingers until the segments are sewn together.

quilts *from* sweet jane

easy quilt patterns using precuts

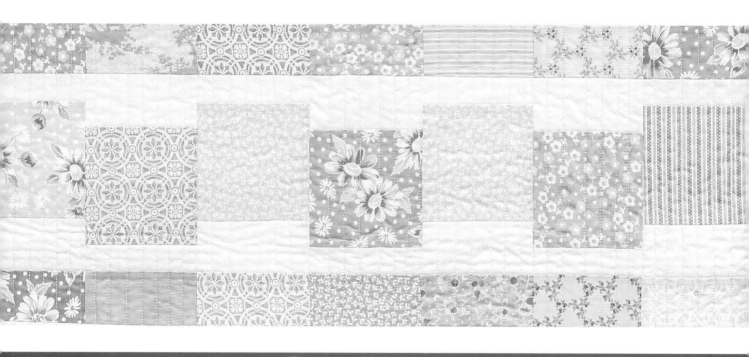

SUE PFAU

Martingale®
Create with Confidence

Quilts from Sweet Jane:
Easy Quilt Patterns using Precuts
© 2013 by Sue Pfau

Martingale®
19021 120th Ave. NE, Ste. 102
Bothell, WA 98011-9511 USA
ShopMartingale.com

Mission Statement

Dedicated to providing quality products and service to inspire creativity.

Credits

PRESIDENT & CEO: Tom Wierzbicki

EDITOR IN CHIEF: Mary V. Green

DESIGN DIRECTOR: Paula Schlosser

MANAGING EDITOR: Karen Costello Soltys

ACQUISITIONS EDITOR: Karen M. Burns

TECHNICAL EDITOR: Ellen Pahl

COPY EDITOR: Tiffany Mottet

PRODUCTION MANAGER: Regina Girard

ILLUSTRATOR: Lisa Lauch

COVER & TEXT DESIGNER: Paula Schlosser

PHOTOGRAPHER: Brent Kane

Printed in China

18 17 16 15 14   8 7 6 5 4 3

Library of Congress Cataloging-in-Publication Data is available upon request.

ISBN: 978-1-60468-270-0

contents

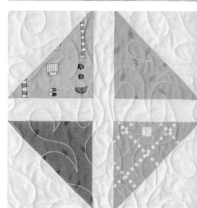

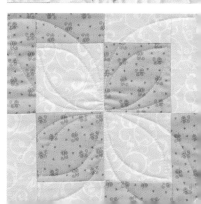

introduction

The patterns in this book are designed to use all or part of one precut bundle of fabric with the addition of some white fabric, or a neutral fabric of your choice. The fabric requirements are so simple that you can start sewing right away! Most of the patterns are easy enough for the beginning quilter; all of them are fast, easy, and fun to make.

If you are looking for a weekend project, or want to use up some of the Jelly Rolls and Layer Cakes sitting in your sewing room, this book will give you many great patterns to choose from. There are even a few baby quilt patterns you can make in just one day.

If you don't use precuts, use your stash fabric! Many of the patterns are perfect for scraps. I hope you enjoy using this book and come back to it again and again!

Pressing is key to making blocks fit nicely when you put your quilt together. To press your segments, put the iron down and pick it up. Do not move the iron over the surface of the fabric. There are different opinions on the subject of steam. I use my iron with steam to press my seams. You need to be careful not to distort the fabric, but you do want to press it so it lies flat when you are done. Make sure that the seam allowances are flat and that there are no "pleats" or creases in the fabric on the right side, or your segments and/or blocks may end up smaller than they should be.

Double-Check for Success

Check the measurement of your finished block and trim it to the correct size. This step is important. If you trim your blocks, they will sew together nicely and your quilt top should be flat. You can measure and trim *sections* of your block or the full block after it goes together. You just need to be sure to trim your block evenly and keep it in proportion. Use both the vertical and horizontal lines on the ruler to ensure you are trimming the block squarely. You may have more excess on one side of the block than the other, so you should never trim the edges without measuring first. For example, if you have a block that should measure 10" square, but it's a bit large, place the 5" intersection of your ruler where the block center should be. Trim the right and top edges. Rotate the block 180° and align the 10" lines of your ruler with the newly cut edges of the block. Trim any excess fabric.

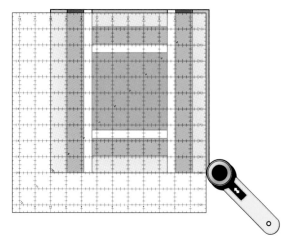

It's always a good idea to make one block before starting your project. You can do this with extra fabric from your project or fabric from your stash. This helps to answer any questions you may have about measurements, cutting, how the blocks go together, etc. If you make a mistake, you will see it and be able to fix it before you ruin the whole quilt!

Adding Sashing and Borders

If the sashing or border pieces are longer than 42", sew the strips together end to end to make one long strip. I like to sew the strips together using a diagonal seam because it seems less noticeable. Refer to "Binding Your Quilt" on page 8 for an illustration of sewing diagonal seams. Once you have a long strip, measure through the center of your quilt and cut the strips to that same measurement. Never measure along the edges of your quilt, because they may actually be longer than the middle due to stretching. Measuring through the middle and cutting the borders to that length will ensure that your quilt is square and flat.

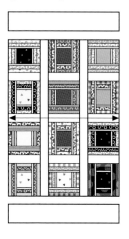 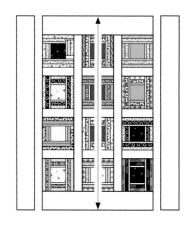

After your border pieces are cut to the correct measurement, fold both the quilt and the border strip in half. Crease the folds with your fingernail to mark the centers. Place the border on the quilt with right sides together, matching the ends and the center creases. Pin these points. There is a good chance that your border strip won't be exactly the same length as your quilt. This is normal! Sew the quilt and border together with the longer section on the bottom, and gently hold the two pieces taut as they go through the sewing machine. The feed dogs should ease the excess fabric through the machine.

Finishing Your Quilt

Once your quilt top is done, you must layer it with the backing and batting into what is called a "quilt sandwich." Cut the batting so that it extends beyond each edge by about 4". Piece together the backing and cut it down so it also extends beyond all four edges of the quilt by at least 4". When you are trimming the backing, make sure the edges are straight when it's finished.

Quilt by hand, quilt by machine, or tie the layers of your quilt together as desired before attaching the binding. There isn't enough space in this book to include detailed information about this process, so refer to some of the many excellent books on the subject, take a class at your favorite quilt shop, or visit ShopMartingale.com/HowtoQuilt for free, downloadable instructions on layering, quilting, binding, and much more.

Binding Your Quilt

The patterns in this book assume a 2½"-wide binding cut on the straight grain. Join the binding strips into one long strip using a diagonal seam. Press each seam allowance open.

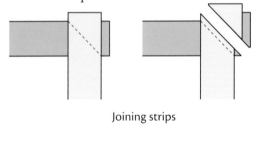

Joining strips

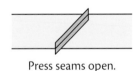

Press seams open.

1. Make the binding long enough to fit around the entire quilt plus at least 12" extra.
2. Press the binding in half lengthwise, wrong sides together.
3. Attach the binding to the quilt. Start by placing the end of the binding strip at a midpoint of one side of the quilt. Make sure the cut edges of the binding are aligned with the cut edges of the quilt. Leave an 8" tail unsewn. Start stitching on the binding with a ¼" seam allowance. Sew to about ¼" from the corner of the quilt and backstitch to secure the thread.

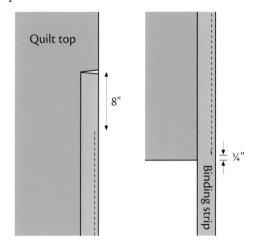

4. Remove the quilt from under the presser foot. Fold the binding over itself to form a 45° angle to the sewn section. Fold the binding back down over the 45° angle, hiding the angle and aligning the strip with the next side of the quilt.

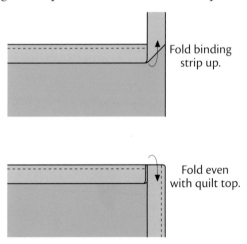

5. Start sewing at the edge of the quilt and sew to ¼" from the next corner, then repeat step 4. Repeat this process until you arrive at the side of the quilt where you started. Sew the binding until you are about 12" to 14" from the beginning stitches. Remove the quilt from your machine.

6. Align the two binding strips together going in opposite directions. Trim the ends so they overlap and you have ¼" of extra fabric on each side of the binding.

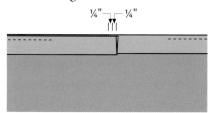

Trim ¼" longer on each end.

7. Unfold the binding strips and pull the ends away from the quilt. Place the ends right sides together. Stitch the ends together with a ¼" seam allowance and finger-press open.

Stitch ends together.

8. Refold the binding and align it with the unstitched edge of the quilt. Stitch the remaining section of the binding to the quilt.

9. Fold the binding to the back of the quilt. The binding will cover the raw edges of the quilt and the stitching on the back of the quilt. Hand stitch the binding in place.

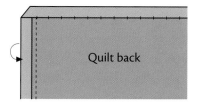

Quilt back

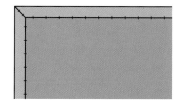

Put Those Scraps to Good Use!

I am a practical person, so fabric scraps really bug me. That's one reason why I love precuts—*fewer scraps!* But they still accumulate. I want to share a few of the ways I use up my scraps.

Make a small quilt. Make a doll quilt for a little girl, or a baby quilt for charity. Many times you can make up four blocks, separate them with 3"-wide sashing and add a 3"- to 4"-wide border. Voilà, you have an awesome little quilt. See pages 25 and 29 for my examples.

Make a table runner. Sew four blocks together end to end. Generally I put a 2½"- to 3½"-wide border around the blocks, depending on their size.

Make a binding. Most of the quilts in this book are scrappy, so making a scrappy pieced binding is a nice fit. Generally you need from five to seven Jelly Roll strips to make a binding for the quilts in this book.

Make a pieced backing. This is my favorite use of leftover blocks, precuts, pieced strips, or fabrics from my stash. Say your quilt is just a few inches wider than the width of the backing fabric. For example, your quilt is 46" wide, and the fabric is 42" wide. Instead of buying two times the length of fabric to make the backing, buy just one length. Make the backing fabric wider by piecing together a variety of fabrics until you have a piece about 10" wide and the same length as your backing. If you are using precuts, generally you need about six to eight Layer Cake squares, or seven or eight Jelly Roll strips.

Cut the backing fabric *lengthwise* (parallel to the selvage edges) into two pieces, as shown in the diagram. There's no need to measure, just make sure the cut is off center. It's more visually pleasing this way and you don't have to worry about keeping it centered. Sew the pieced section between the two backing pieces. Press the seam allowances open to minimize bulk. Your backing should now be at least 50" wide. Trim the edges to square up the backing, and it's ready for the quilt sandwich!

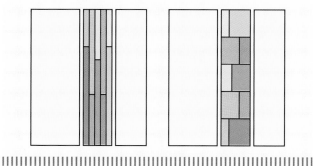

Pieced and quilted by Sue Pfau | Finished quilt: 65½" x 78½" | Finished block: 12" x 12"

modern greek cross

I added a small twist to the traditional setting of this Greek Cross block, and I love how it turned out! Sometimes a little sashing is all you need to reinvent a classic favorite. This quilt is a large lap quilt or excellent coverlet for a twin or full bed. Because the blocks are simple, this quilt comes together very quickly.

Materials

Yardage is based on 42"-wide fabric, unless otherwise noted.

30 Layer Cake squares, 10" x 10", for blocks

2½ yards of white fabric for blocks, sashing, and inner border

1½ yards of fabric for outer border

⅔ yard of fabric for binding

4¼ yards of fabric for backing

74" x 87" piece of batting

Cutting

From the white fabric, cut:
   10 strips, 2½" x 42"; crosscut into 80 rectangles, 2½" x 4½"
   5 strips, 5" x 42"; crosscut into 40 squares, 5" x 5"
   11 strips, 1½" x 42"; crosscut *5 of the strips* into 16 strips, 1½" x 12½"
   7 strips, 2" x 42"

From *each of 10* of the 10" squares for block corners, cut:
   4 squares, 5" x 5"

From *each of 20* of the 10" squares for block centers, cut:
   1 rectangle, 4½" x 8½"
   2 rectangles, 2½" x 4½"

From the outer-border fabric, cut:
   8 strips, 6" x 42"

From the binding fabric, cut:
   8 strips, 2½" x 42"

Piecing the Blocks

1. Draw a diagonal line from corner to corner on the *wrong* side of each white 5" square. Match up each of these squares with a colored 5" square, right sides together. Sew a scant ¼" seam on each side of the diagonal line. Cut each square in half along the diagonal line and press the seam allowances toward the darker fabric. You'll have two identical half-square-triangle units. Repeat for all of the 5" squares to make a total of 80 half-square-triangle units.

Make 80.

2. Trim each half-square-triangle unit to measure 4½" x 4½" as follows. Line up the diagonal line on the ruler with the diagonal seam on the unit. Before making your first cut, make sure all of the edges of the unit hang over the 4½" marks on the ruler or are flush with them. Trim the top and right edges of the unit. Rotate the unit 180°. Align the 4½" marks on the ruler to be

flush with the cut edges of the unit. Trim the top and right edges of the unit.

3. Sew white 2½" x 4½" rectangles to opposite sides of a 4½" x 8½" rectangle. Press the seam allowances toward the darker fabric. Make 20.

Make 20.

4. Sew two matching 2½" x 4½" rectangles and two white 2½" x 4½" rectangles in pairs lengthwise. Press the seam allowances toward the darker fabric. Make 40.

Make 40.

5. Assemble each block as shown, using matching units from steps 3 and 4 and four matching half-square-triangle units that complement the block center. The block should measure 12½" square; trim if necessary.

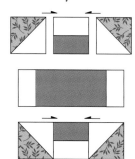

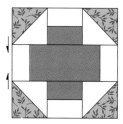

Make 20.

Assembling the Quilt Top

1. Arrange the blocks in four vertical rows of five blocks each. Refer to the assembly diagram on the opposite page.
2. Add a white 1½" x 12½" sashing strip between the blocks in each vertical row.
3. Sew the blocks and sashing strips into four vertical rows. Press the seam allowances toward the blocks.
4. Join the white 1½" x 42" sashing strips end to end into one long strip. Measure the vertical rows of the quilt, determine the average measurement, and cut three sashing strips to this length. Sew the sashing strips and vertical rows together. Press the seam allowances toward the rows.

Adding the Borders

1. Join the white 2" x 42" inner-border strips end to end into one long strip. Measure the length of the quilt through the center and trim two strips to that measurement. Sew these strips to the sides of the quilt. Press the seam allowances toward the quilt center. Repeat to measure, trim, and add the inner border to the top and bottom of the quilt.
2. Join the 6" x 42" outer-border strips into one long strip using diagonal seams (shown on page 8). Repeat step 1 to add the outer borders to the quilt. Press the seam allowances toward the outer border.

Finishing the Quilt

1. Cut and piece the backing fabric so it's 4" larger than the quilt top on all sides. Cut the batting approximately the same size.
2. Mark any quilting lines needed, then layer the backing, batting, and quilt top. Baste the layers together and quilt as desired.
3. Trim the backing and batting even with the quilt top, using your 24" quilting ruler, rotary cutter, and mat.
4. Make and attach the binding, referring to "Binding Your Quilt" on page 8 as needed.

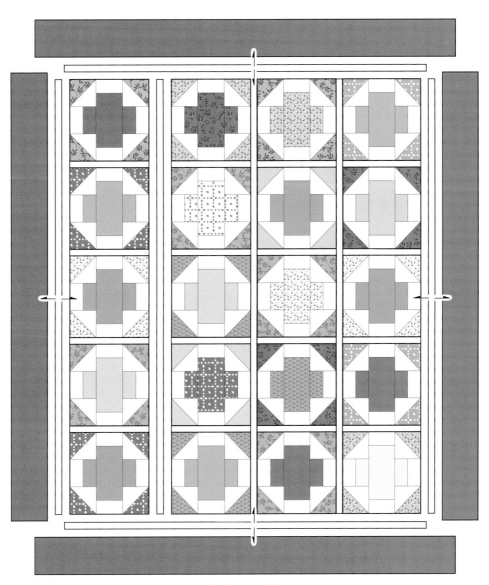

Quilt assembly

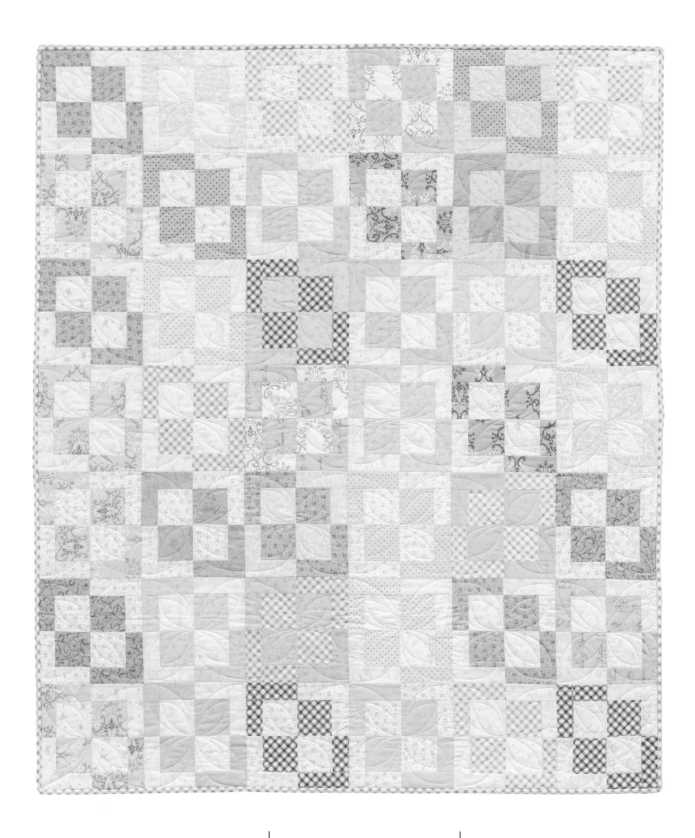

Pieced and quilted by Sue Pfau | Finished quilt: 48½" x 56½" | Finished block: 8" x 8"

penny lane

This quilt was great fun to make. I simply sewed a big Four Patch block, cut it up, and sewed it back together again! You can use any Layer Cake bundle, or cut your own squares. I enjoyed making this quilt so much that I made two different versions. See the photograph on page 16 and look how differently they turned out!

Materials

Yardage is based on 42"-wide fabric, unless otherwise noted.

42 Layer Cake squares, 10" x 10", for blocks

½ yard of fabric for binding

3¼ yards of fabric for backing*

57" x 65" piece of batting

If you want to purchase less backing and use up some scraps, this is a perfect quilt to try my pieced backing suggestion on page 9.

Cutting

From *each* of the 10" squares, cut:
   4 squares, 5" x 5" (168 total)

From the binding fabric, cut:
   6 strips, 2½" x 42"

Piecing the Blocks

1. Select two contrasting pairs of matching 5" squares. Sew the squares together into a four-patch unit. Press the seam allowances toward the darker fabric.

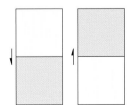 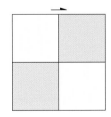

2. Cut 1¾"-wide strips off opposite sides of the four-patch unit, in the order shown. You will be left with a 6" x 6" four-patch unit.

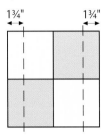

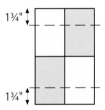

3. Trim the longer strips so they measure 4¼" on each side of the center seam. (They should measure 8½" long.)

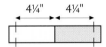

4. Sew the shorter 1¾"-wide strips back onto the top and bottom of the block, rotating the strips so that contrasting fabrics are joined. Press the seam allowances toward the center of the block. Sew the longer strips to the sides of the block. Press the seam allowances toward the left side of the block. The finished block should measure

8½" square; trim if necessary. If you trim the block, be sure to keep the middle seam at 4¼" on your ruler.

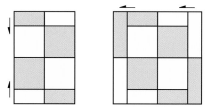

5. Repeat steps 1–4 to make a total of 42 blocks.

Assembling the Quilt Top

1. Arrange the blocks in seven horizontal rows of six blocks each. I laid them out so the darker corners are always in the upper-left and lower-right corners of the blocks. Rotate the blocks 180° as needed so that the seam allowances will butt against each other nicely.

2. Sew the blocks together into rows. Press the seam allowances in opposite directions from row to row. Join the rows. Press the seam allowances in the same direction.

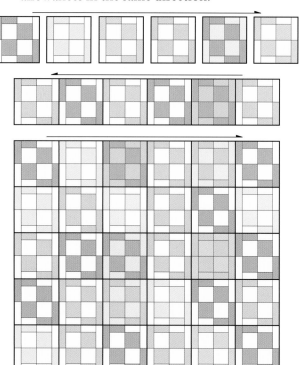

Quilt assembly

Finishing the Quilt

1. Cut and piece the backing fabric so it's 4" larger than the quilt top on all sides. Cut the batting approximately the same size.

2. Mark any quilting lines needed, then layer the backing, batting, and quilt top. Baste the layers together and quilt as desired.

3. Trim the backing and batting even with the quilt top, using your 24" quilting ruler, rotary cutter, and mat.

4. Make and attach the binding, referring to "Binding Your Quilt" on page 8 as needed.

Color Option

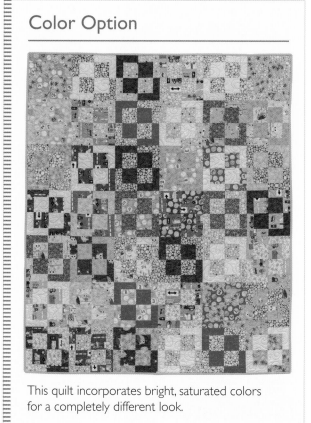

This quilt incorporates bright, saturated colors for a completely different look.

under the sea

This quilt is intriguing because it's made of just one block, but when put together, the blocks form three different designs on the quilt. I love the bold geometric shapes mixed with a scrappy look.

Materials

Yardage is based on 42"-wide fabric, unless otherwise noted.

38 Jelly Roll strips, 2½" x 44", for blocks and pieced border

3 yards of white fabric for blocks and borders

⅔ yard of fabric for binding

4¾ yards of fabric for backing

69" x 85" piece of batting

Cutting

From *each of 20* of the 2½"-wide strips, cut:
    1 strip, 2½" x 13" (20 total)
    5 rectangles, 2½" x 4½" (100 total; 4 are extra)

From the remaining scraps and 2½"-wide strips, cut:
    48 rectangles, 2½" x 5½"
    32 strips, 2½" x 10¼"

From the white fabric, cut:
    26 strips, 2½" x 42"; crosscut into:
        96 rectangles, 2½" x 4½"
        20 strips, 2½" x 13"
        48 rectangles, 2½" x 5½"
    13 strips, 2½" x 42", for border

From the binding fabric, cut:
    8 strips, 2½" x 42"

The Perfect Jelly Roll

When you are trying to pick the perfect Jelly Roll for your project, don't overlook batiks! Batiks come in precut bundles, and the colors are so rich and beautiful! One great thing about batiks is they don't have very many light strips in them, so they fit perfectly with the patterns in this book.

Piecing the Blocks

1. Sew a colored 2½" x 13" strip to a white 2½" x 13" strip lengthwise. Make 20 strip sets and cut them into 96 segments, 2½" wide.

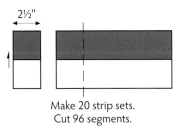

2½"

Make 20 strip sets.
Cut 96 segments.

Cutting Straight

When cutting strip sets into smaller segments, align one of the lines on your ruler with a seam of the strip set. This way you will have a "squared off" cut every time.

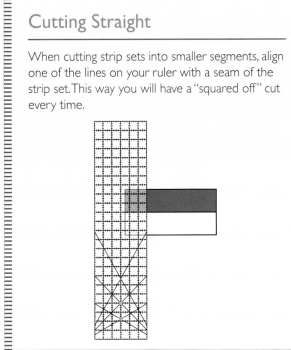

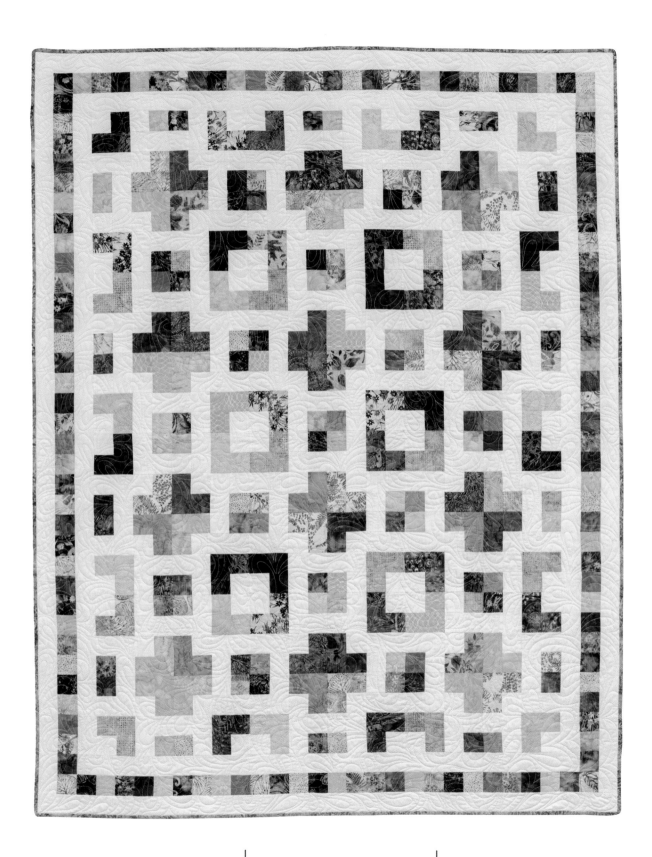

Pieced and quilted by Sue Pfau | Finished quilt: 60½" x 76½" | Finished block: 16" x 16"

2. Sew a matching 2½" x 4½" rectangle to the segment from step 1 to make unit A. Make sure the pieced segment is on the right with the white square on top. Press the seam allowances toward the rectangle. Make 96 units. *Sew each one exactly the same.*

Unit A.
Make 96.

3. Sew a colored 2½" x 5½" rectangle to a white 2½" x 5½" rectangle along the long edges as shown. Make 48 strip sets and cut them into 96 segments, 2½" wide.

2½"

Make 48 strip sets.
Cut 96 segments.

4. Sew a white 2½" x 4½" rectangle to the segment from step 3 to make unit B. Make sure the pieced segment is on the right with the white square on top. Press the seam allowances toward the pieced segment. Make 96 units. *Sew each one exactly the same.*

Unit B.
Make 96.

5. Sew a unit A and a unit B together exactly as shown. Press the seam allowances away from the white rectangle. Make 48.

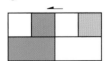

Make 48.

6. Sew a unit A and a unit B together exactly as shown. Press the seam allowances away from the white rectangle. Make 48.

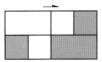

Make 48.

7. Sew one unit from step 5 and one unit from step 6 together as shown to make a quarter of a block. Make 48.

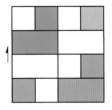

Make 48.

Taming Tricky Seams

If the seam allowances are pressed in the same directions when you sew the segments or blocks of this quilt together, pin them in the opposite direction. Then, after you sew the segments together, snip the fabric in the seam allowances just below the sewn intersection and press the seam allowances back to their original position.

8. Sew four quarter blocks together exactly as shown. Make 12 blocks. The blocks should measure 16½" square.

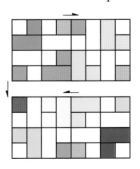
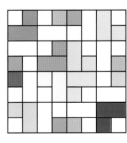

Make 12.

Assembling the Quilt Top

Arrange the blocks in four horizontal rows of three blocks each. Sew the blocks into rows. Press the seam allowances in opposite directions from row to row. Join the rows and press in the same direction.

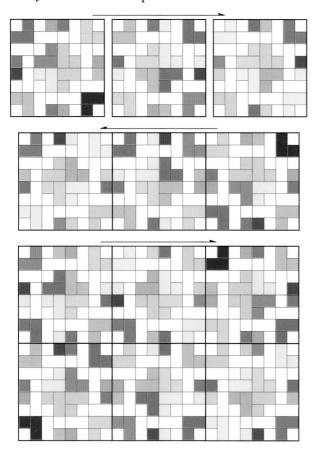

Adding the Borders

1. Join six white 2½" x 42" strips end to end using diagonal seams (shown on page 8). Cut two strips, 2½" x 64½", and two strips, 2½" x 52½". Sew the longer strips to the sides of the quilt. Press the seam allowances toward the quilt center. Sew the shorter strips to the top and bottom of the quilt. Press toward the quilt center.

2. Sew the 2½" x 10¼" strips together lengthwise in pairs, creating many different color combinations. Press the seam allowances toward the darker fabrics. Make 16 strip sets and cut them into 62 segments, 2½" wide, for the pieced border.

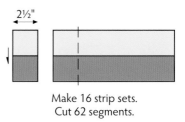

Make 16 strip sets.
Cut 62 segments.

3. Join 17 border segments end to end for each long side of the quilt. Sew them to the sides of the quilt. Press the seam allowances toward the pieced border.

4. Join 14 border segments end to end for the top and bottom of the quilt. Sew to the quilt. Press the seam allowances toward the pieced border.

5. Join the remaining seven white 2½" x 42" strips end to end using diagonal seams. Cut two strips, 2½" x 72½", and two strips, 2½" x 60½".

6. Sew the longer strips to the sides of the quilt. Press the seam allowances toward the quilt center. Sew the shorter strips to the top and bottom of the quilt. Press the seam allowances toward the pieced border.

Finishing the Quilt

1. Cut and piece the backing fabric so it's 4" larger than the quilt top on all sides. Cut the batting approximately the same size.
2. Mark any quilting lines needed, then layer the backing, batting, and quilt top. Baste the layers together and quilt as desired.
3. Trim the backing and batting even with the quilt top, using your 24" quilting ruler, rotary cutter, and mat.
4. Make and attach the binding, referring to "Binding Your Quilt" on page 8 as needed.

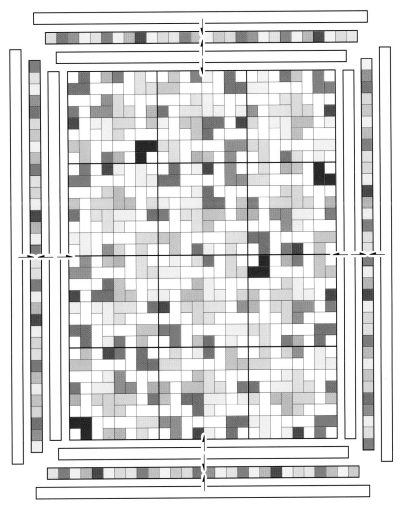

Quilt assembly

Pieced by Abby Sisk;
quilted by Jennifer Krohn

Finished quilt: 45" x 57"

Finished block: 9½" x 9½"

red-letter day

This is a somewhat sophisticated, modern quilt that comes together quickly. I just love the graphic look of the simple, bold blocks surrounded by white. I think this quilt would look stunning with a gray or black background as well.

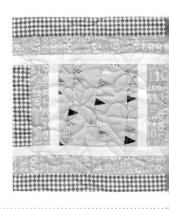

Materials

Yardage is based on 42"-wide fabric, unless otherwise noted.

15 to 20 Layer Cake squares, 10" x 10", for blocks

1⅞ yards of white fabric for blocks, sashing, and border

½ yard of fabric for binding

3¼ yards of fabric for backing*

53" x 65" piece of batting

If you want to purchase less backing and use up some scraps, this is a perfect quilt to try my pieced backing suggestion on page 9.

Cutting

From *each of 6* of the 10" squares for block centers, cut:

2 squares, 5" x 5" (12 total)

From the remaining 10" squares, cut:

24 matching sets of 3 strips, 1½" x 10" (72 total)

From the white fabric, cut:

5 strips, 6" x 42"

3 strips, 3" x 42"; crosscut into 9 strips, 3" x 10"

3 strips, 3" x 42"

12 strips, 1" x 42"

From the binding fabric, cut:

6 strips, 2½" x 42"

If Bigger Is Better

This quilt can easily be made bigger. Each additional block needs one 5" square and two sets of three matching 1½" × 10" strips. You'll also need additional white fabric.

Piecing the Blocks

1. Choose two complementary sets of three 1½" x 10" strips. Sew them together lengthwise to make three identical strip sets. Press the seam allowances toward the darker fabric.

Make 3.

2. Sew the 10" strip sets lengthwise to a white 1" x 42" strip. Press the seam allowances toward the darker fabric. Cut through the white strip to make three 10" segments. Cut one of the segments into two segments, 5" wide. Keep the other two intact.

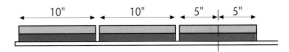

3. Sew the two 5"-wide segments to opposite sides of a 5" square, placing the white strip next to the square. Press the seam allowances toward the square.

4. Sew 10"-long segments to opposite sides of the unit from step 3, placing the white strip next to the center unit. Press the seam allowances toward the block center. Repeat the steps to make 12 blocks.

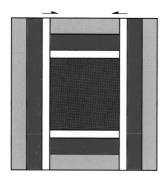

Make 12.

Assembling the Quilt Top

1. Arrange the blocks in three vertical rows of four blocks each. Alternate each block so that the longer white strips are horizontal in one and vertical in the next.

2. Sew a white 3" x 10" strip to the bottom of the top three blocks in each vertical row. Press the seam allowances toward the blocks.

3. Sew the blocks together into three vertical rows, pressing the seam allowances toward the blocks.

4. Join the white 3" x 42" strips end to end using diagonal seams (shown on page 8). Measure the length of the vertical rows and cut two strips to this length. Sew the vertical rows together with the sashing strips. Press the seam allowances toward the blocks.

5. Measure the width of the quilt through the center and cut two white 6" x 42" strips to this width. Sew to the top and bottom of the quilt. Press the seam allowances toward the quilt center.

6. Join the three remaining white 6" x 42" strips end to end using diagonal seams. Measure the length of the quilt through the center and cut two strips to this length. Sew to the sides of the quilt. Press the seam allowances toward the quilt center.

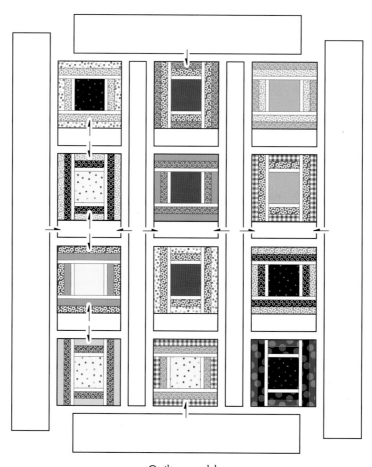

Quilt assembly

Finishing the Quilt

1. Cut and piece the backing fabric so it's 4" larger than the quilt top on all sides. Cut the batting approximately the same size.
2. Mark any quilting lines needed, then layer the backing, batting, and quilt top. Baste the layers together and quilt as desired.
3. Trim the backing and batting even with the quilt top, using your 24" quilting ruler, rotary cutter, and mat.
4. Make and attach the binding, referring to "Binding Your Quilt" on page 8 as needed.

Size Option

I used some scraps to create this cute doll quilt. The sashing and borders are all 3" wide.

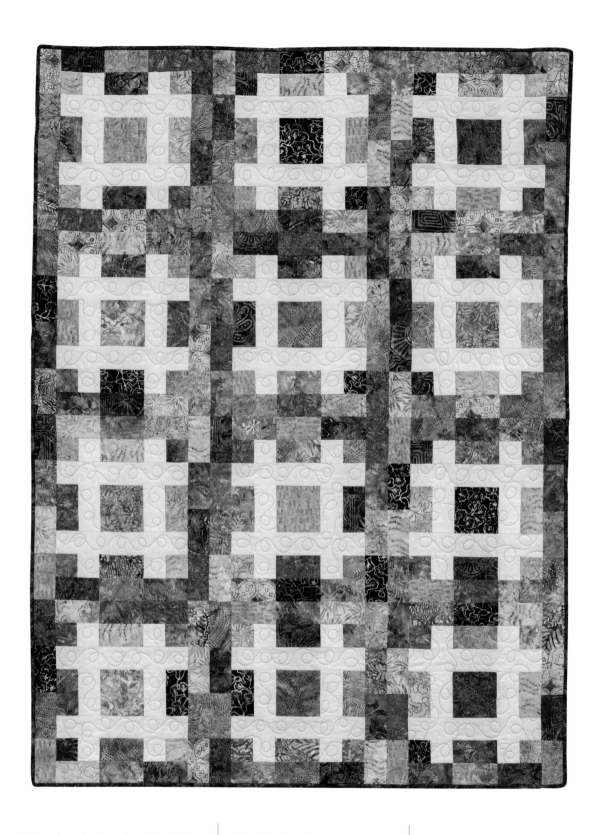

Pieced and quilted by Sue Pfau | Finished quilt: 48½" x 64½" | Finished block: 16" x 16"

pound cake

This is an awesome scrap quilt. It would also look fabulous using all different shades and prints of the same color. In this pattern, I wanted to play with color placement, so I reversed the typical placement of light and dark colors—allowing the darks to create the background and the cream fabric to feature the design.

Materials

Yardage is based on 42"-wide fabric, unless otherwise noted.

33 to 40 medium to dark Layer Cake squares, 10" x 10", for blocks

1¼ yards of cream fabric for blocks

½ yard of fabric for binding

3¼ yards of fabric for backing*

57" x 73" piece of batting

If you want to purchase less backing and use up some scraps, this is a perfect quilt to try my pieced backing suggestion on page 9.

Cutting

From *each of 6* medium or dark 10" squares for block centers, cut:

2 squares, 4½" x 4½" (12 total)

From *each of 12* medium or dark 10" squares, cut:

2 strips, 2½" x 10" (24 total)

From the remaining 10" squares and scraps, cut *a total of*:

192 rectangles, 2½" x 4½"

From the cream fabric, cut:

8 strips, 2½" x 42"; crosscut into 24 strips, 2½" x 12½"

6 strips, 2½" x 42"; crosscut into 24 strips, 2½" x 10"

From the binding fabric, cut:

6 strips, 2½" x 42"

Piecing the Blocks

1. Sew a medium or dark 2½" x 10" strip to a cream 2½" x 10" strip lengthwise. Press the seam allowances toward the darker fabric. Make 24 strip sets. Cut each strip set into two 2½"-wide segments and one 4½"-wide segment.

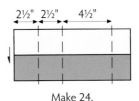

Make 24.

2. Sew 4½"-wide segments to opposite sides of a medium or dark 4½" square, placing the cream rectangle next to the square. Press the seam allowances toward the square. Make 12.

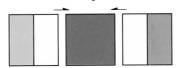

Make 12.

Sorting the Squares

I strongly advise you to use dark and medium fabrics around the cream. You can put some of your lighter fabrics in the outer frame of the block, but they still need to contrast with the cream fabric. You really want a contrast around the "pound signs."

3. Sew 2½"-wide segments to opposite sides of a medium or dark 2½" x 4½" rectangle, placing the cream square next to the rectangle. Press the seam allowances toward the rectangle. Make 24.

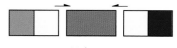

Make 24.

4. Sew a cream 2½" x 12½" strip lengthwise to each unit from step 3. Press the seam allowances toward the pieced unit. Make 24.

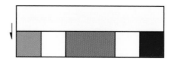

Make 24.

5. Sew units from step 4 to opposite sides of the center units from step 2, placing the cream strips next to the center unit. Press the seam allowances toward the center of the block. Each block should measure 12½" square; trim if necessary.

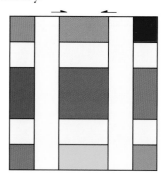

Make 12.

6. Join the remaining 2½" x 4½" rectangles end to end to make 24 sets of three rectangles and 24 sets of four rectangles. Press the seam allowances as shown.

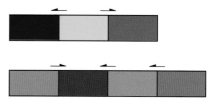

Make 24 of each.

7. Sew three-rectangle units to opposite sides of each of the blocks from step 5. Be sure to keep the pound sign aligned the same for each block. Press the seam allowances toward the three-rectangle units.

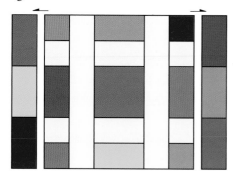

8. Sew a four-rectangle unit to the top and bottom of each block. Press the seam allowances toward the four-rectangle units.

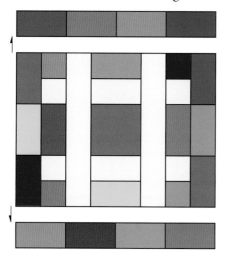

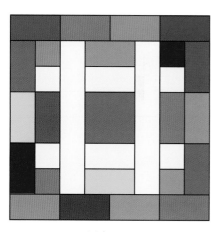

Make 12.

Assembling the Quilt Top

1. Arrange the blocks in four rows of three blocks each. Try to avoid placing the same colors next to each other. Also, keep your pound signs aligned in the same direction in each block. I liked the look of the pound signs and rectangle units all going in the same direction, but I did pin and snip the seam allowances to do this (see "Taming Tricky Seams" on page 19). If you prefer to rotate the blocks, the seam allowances should butt against each other.

2. Sew the blocks into rows. Press the seam allowances in opposite directions from row to row. Join the rows and press in the same direction.

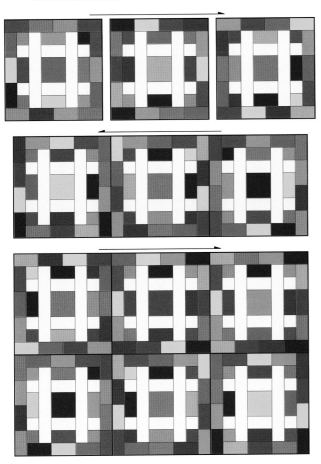

Quilt assembly

Finishing the Quilt

1. Cut and piece the backing fabric so it's 4" larger than the quilt top on all sides. Cut the batting approximately the same size.

2. Mark any quilting lines needed, then layer the backing, batting, and quilt top. Baste the layers together and quilt as desired.

3. Trim the backing and batting even with the quilt top, using your 24" quilting ruler, rotary cutter, and mat.

4. Make and attach the binding, referring to "Binding Your Quilt" on page 8 as needed.

Color Option

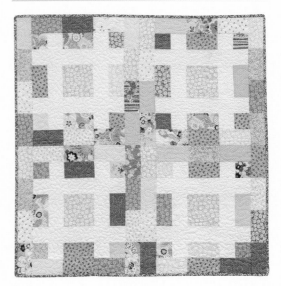

I made a little baby quilt with some leftovers from another project. I wanted to see how this quilt would look made with lighter fabrics.

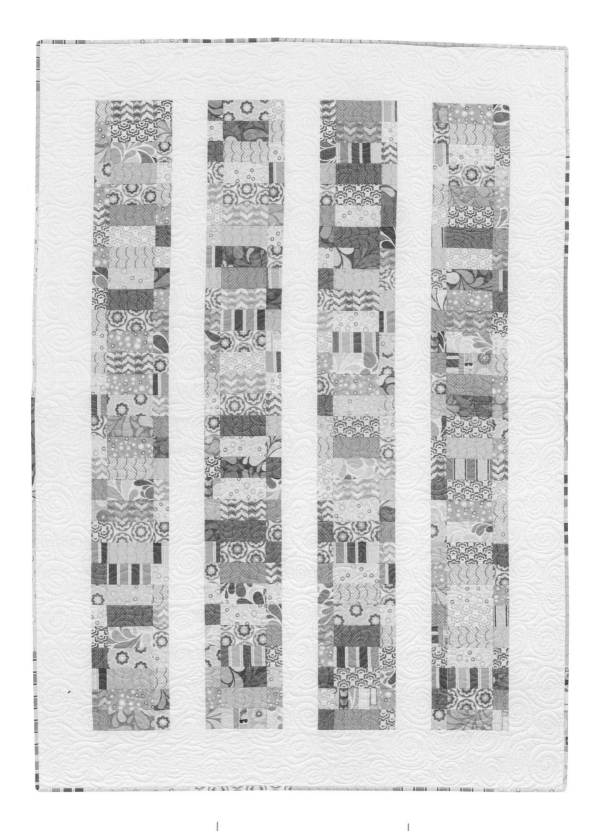

Pieced and quilted by Sue Pfau | Finished quilt: 54" x 71½" | Finished block: 8" x 12"

my garden trellis

I love Stacked Coin quilts. They are a perfect outlet for using up scraps. This quilt is fun, quick, and easy to make! It would make an excellent beginner quilt or a quick quilt for charity.

Materials

Yardage is based on 42"-wide fabric, unless otherwise noted.

30 to 35 Layer Cake squares, 10" x 10", *or* 30 to 35 Jelly Roll strips, 2½" x 42", for blocks

2 yards of white fabric for sashing and border

⅝ yard of fabric for binding

3½ yards of fabric for backing

62" x 80" piece of batting

Cutting

From the 10" squares or 2½"-wide strips, cut *a total of*:

120 strips, 2½" x 10"

From the white fabric, cut from the *lengthwise* grain*:

3 strips, 4" x length of fabric
4 strips, 6" x length of fabric

From the binding fabric, cut:

7 strips, 2½" x 42"

*You can wait until your quilt blocks have been pieced to cut the borders to fit.

Scrappy Binding

I purchased a Layer Cake of 42 squares for this quilt and used the leftover 10" squares for the binding. I sewed 26 strips, 2½" × 10", together end to end. If you use Jelly Roll strips, you will need only seven strips.

Piecing the Blocks

1. Sew six 2½" x 10" strips together lengthwise. When sewing the strip sets together, try to put a variety of colors and prints in each set. Press the seam allowances in the same direction. Make 20 strip sets.

Make 20 strip sets.

2. Cut each of the strip sets into one 5½"-wide segment and two 2"-wide segments.

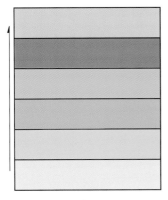

3. Sew random 2" x 12½" segments to opposite sides of a 5½" x 12½" segment. Nest the seam allowances together so the corners match up nicely. Press the seam allowances toward the block center. Make 20 blocks.

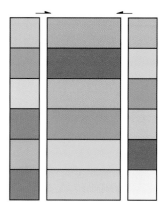

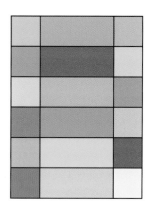

Make 20.

Assembling the Quilt Top

1. Arrange the blocks into four vertical rows of five blocks each. Sew the blocks into vertical rows and press in the same direction.
2. Measure the length of the rows and determine the average measurement (it should be 60½"). Trim the three white 4"-wide sashing strips *and* two of the white 6"-wide border strips to the same average length of the vertical rows.
3. Sew the vertical block rows together with the 4"-wide sashing strips. Press the seam allowances toward the blocks.
4. Sew the 6"-wide border strips from step 2 to the sides of the quilt. Press the seam allowances toward the quilt center.

5. Measure the width of the quilt through the center; it should be 54". Trim the remaining 6"-wide border strips to this measurement. Sew to the top and bottom of the quilt. Press the seam allowances toward the quilt center.

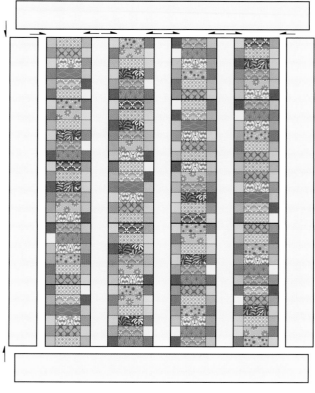

Quilt assembly

Finishing the Quilt

1. Cut and piece the backing fabric so it's 4" larger than the quilt top on all sides. Cut the batting approximately the same size.
2. Mark any quilting lines needed, then layer the backing, batting, and quilt top. Baste the layers together and quilt as desired.
3. Trim the backing and batting even with the quilt top, using your 24" quilting ruler, rotary cutter, and mat.
4. Make and attach the binding, referring to "Binding Your Quilt" on page 8 as needed.

no place like home

Here's another ideal candidate for a scrap quilt. It uses a partial seam, which allows for the fluid movement in the blocks. If you have never sewn a partial seam before, don't let it stop you from making this quilt. It's easy and fun—I promise!

Materials

Yardage is based on 42"-wide fabric, unless otherwise noted.

40 to 42 Layer Cake squares, 10" x 10", for blocks

2⅓ yards of ivory fabric for blocks

⅝ yard of fabric for binding

4 yards of fabric for backing

69" x 81" piece of batting

Sorting the Squares

You should be able to make any Layer Cake bundle work with this pattern. Use lighter squares for the centers of the blocks. Fabrics that contrast nicely with the ivory fabric can be used for the strips that surround the square. You will need 30 Layer Cake squares for the 2½" × 10" strips. Keep in mind that even a busy print with a white or ivory background can make an interesting contrast with the ivory.

Cutting

From *each of 15* lighter 10" squares, cut:

2 squares, 4½" x 4½" (30 total)

From the remaining 10" squares and scraps, cut *a total of*:

120 strips, 2½" x 10"

From the ivory fabric, cut:

30 strips, 2½" x 42"

From the binding fabric, cut:

7 strips, 2½" x 42"

Piecing the Blocks

1. Sew each 2½" x 10" strip lengthwise to the ivory 2½" x 42" strips. Press the seam allowances toward the darker fabric. Cut each of the sewn strips as shown so that the segment measures 8½" wide. Cut 120 segments.

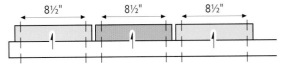

2. Align the edge of one segment with the edge of a 4½" square as shown, right sides together. Make sure that the darker fabric is next to the square. Sew the two pieces together with a partial seam, starting at the aligned edges and stitching about halfway across the square. Press the seam allowances toward the square near the beginning edge only. I usually just finger-press about 1" of the seam allowance. Do not press near the end of the stitching in the middle of the square; doing so will make it harder to complete the seam later.

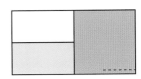

Pieced and quilted by Sue Pfau | Finished quilt: 60½" x 72½" | Finished block: 12" x 12"

3. Sew a second segment to the sewn side of the block. Press the seam allowances toward the square. Working clockwise, add the third and fourth segments in the same manner. All of the segments will fit perfectly and you will sew a complete seam for each.

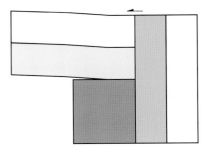

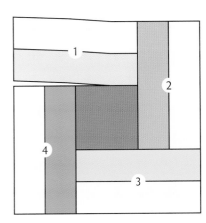

4. To complete the partial seam, fold the partially sewn segment over so that the right sides are together, and align the raw edges on the sides. Make sure everything is nice and flat. Start sewing in the middle of the block, overlapping some of the original stitches. Sew toward the outer edge. The block should measure 12½" square; trim if necessary.

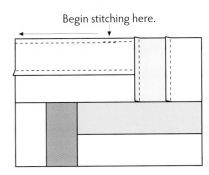

Begin stitching here.

5. Repeat steps 2–4 to make 30 blocks.

Assembling the Quilt Top

1. Arrange the blocks into six horizontal rows of five blocks each. Sew the blocks into rows. Press the seam allowances in opposite directions from row to row.

2. Join the rows and press in the same direction.

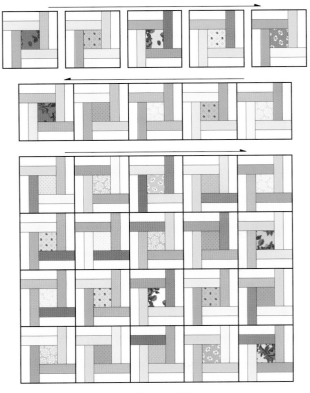

Quilt assembly

Finishing the Quilt

1. Cut and piece the backing fabric so it's 4" larger than the quilt top on all sides. Cut the batting approximately the same size.

2. Mark any quilting lines needed, then layer the backing, batting, and quilt top. Baste the layers together and quilt as desired.

3. Trim the backing and batting even with the quilt top, using your 24" quilting ruler, rotary cutter, and mat.

4. Make and attach the binding, referring to "Binding Your Quilt" on page 8 as needed.

Make a Baby Quilt

Make a sweet baby quilt with just 12 blocks. I used an alternative layout when assembling these blocks. I sewed the strips to the center squares with the white next to the square for a totally different look!

You'll need:

- 12 squares, 4½" x 4½"
- 48 medium print or solid strips, 2½" x 10"
- 12 white strips, 2½" x 42"

Arrange and sew the blocks together in four horizontal rows with three blocks in each row.

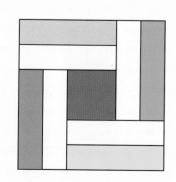

garden blooms

This pattern will work well with just about any Layer Cake bundle. The large blocks lend themselves to large-scale prints, memory quilts, or a space to embroider a customized design. I made this quilt in one day; it's so quick and easy! I would consider this an excellent pattern for a beginner.

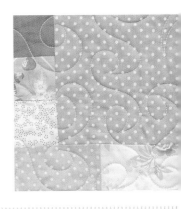

Materials

Yardage is based on 42"-wide fabric, unless otherwise noted.

38 to 40 Layer Cake squares, 10" x 10", for blocks

⅜ yard of fabric for binding

2¾ yards of fabric for backing*

49" x 57" piece of batting

This quilt is 41" wide. The width of a cut of fabric may be sufficient for the backing, assuming it's at least 44" to 45" wide. You could get by with 1⅔ yards of fabric if you piece it using my suggestions on page 9.

Cutting

From *each of 30* Layer Cake squares, cut *in this order*:

    1 strip, 2½" x 10" (30 total); crosscut into
        2 rectangles, 2½" x 4½" (60 total)

    1 square, 6½" x 6½" (30 total)

From the remaining squares and scraps, cut *a total of*:

    18 strips, 2½" x 10"

    12 rectangles, 2½" x 6½"

From the binding fabric, cut:

    5 strips, 2½" x 42"

Piecing the Blocks

Specific pressing instructions for the seam allowances are not given. You can press them however you want—it doesn't matter which way they go.

1. Join the 2½" x 4½" rectangles end to end in pairs. Make 30.

Make 30.

2. Sew three 2½" x 10" strips together lengthwise. Make six strip sets. Cut each strip set into three segments, 2½" wide, for a total of 18 segments.

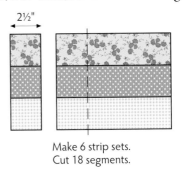

2½"

Make 6 strip sets.
Cut 18 segments.

3. Sew a segment from step 2 to a 6½" square. Make 18.

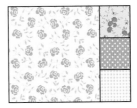

Make 18.

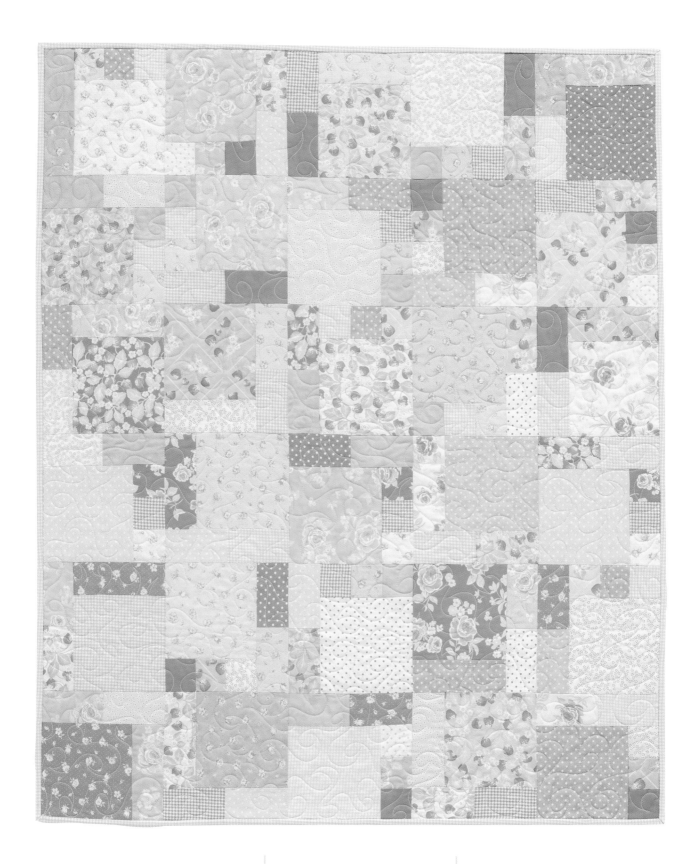

Pieced and quilted by Sue Pfau | Finished quilt: 40½" x 48½" | Finished block: 8" x 8"

4. Sew a 2½" x 6½" rectangle to each remaining 6½" square. Make 12.

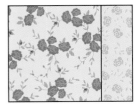

Make 12.

5. Sew a unit from step 1 to the top of each unit from step 3 and step 4 as shown. Be sure to keep the strip segment or rectangle on the right side of the block as you are sewing. The block should measure 8½" square; trim if necessary.

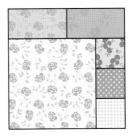

Make 18.

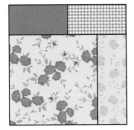

Make 12.

Assembling the Quilt Top

1. Arrange the blocks into six horizontal rows of five blocks each. Lay out the blocks as shown in the quilt assembly diagram or as desired. You may want to experiment with different layouts before sewing the blocks together.

2. Sew the blocks into rows. Press the seam allowances in opposite directions from row to row. Join the rows and press all seam allowances in the same direction.

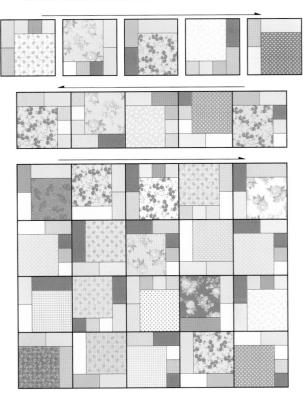

Quilt assembly

Finishing the Quilt

1. Cut and piece the backing fabric so it's 4" larger than the quilt top on all sides. Cut the batting approximately the same size.

2. Mark any quilting lines needed, then layer the backing, batting, and quilt top. Baste the layers together and quilt as desired.

3. Trim the backing and batting even with the quilt top, using your 24" quilting ruler, rotary cutter, and mat.

4. Make and attach the binding, referring to "Binding Your Quilt" on page 8 as needed.

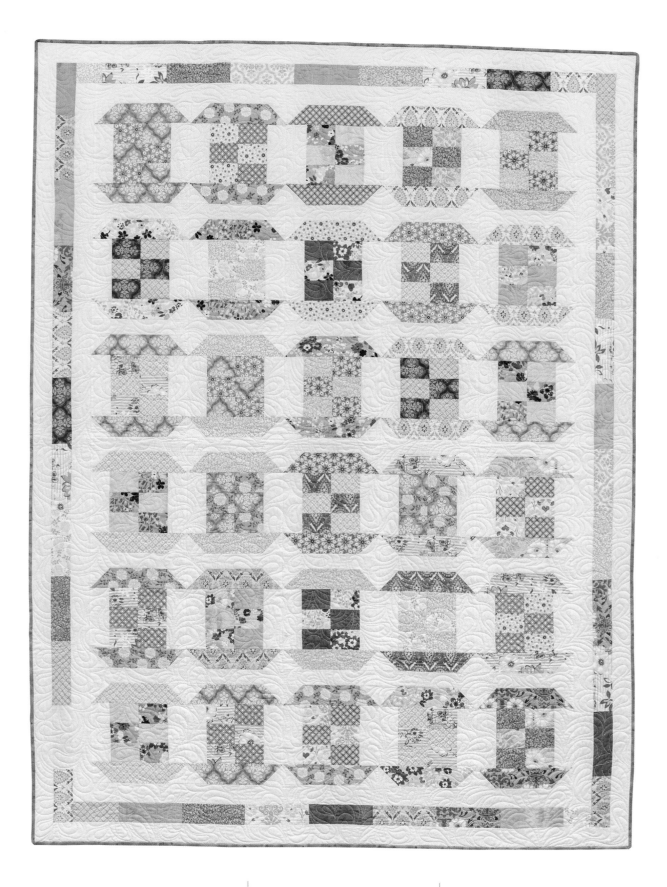

Pieced and quilted by Sue Pfau | Finished quilt: 62½" x 80" | Finished block: 10" x 10"

apple of my eye

This quilt turned out to be a pleasant surprise for me. I was trying to make a Nine Patch quilt and found I didn't have enough material. While playing around with my fabrics, I ended up with this darling block instead! This makes a surprisingly large quilt. It's great for a twin bed, or coverlet for any other size bed. My friend thought the blocks looked like apple cores, so that is how the quilt got its name.

Materials

Yardage is based on 42"-wide fabric, unless otherwise noted.

40 Jelly Roll strips, 2½" x 44", for blocks and pieced border*

3 yards of white fabric for blocks, sashing, and borders

⅔ yard of fabric for binding

5 yards of fabric for backing

69" x 86" piece of batting

Measure your strips before cutting to make sure they're at least 42" long after removing selvages.

Pick the Perfect Jelly Roll

This pattern requires most of the Jelly Roll strips in your bundle. You can use some light strips in the middle of your block, but you should pick a Jelly Roll that has mostly darks, mediums, or "busy" light strips for contrast with the background.

Cutting

From the 2½"-wide strips, cut:

30 *matching pairs* of strips, 2½" x 10½" (60 total)

From the remaining strips and scraps, cut:

30 *matching sets of 3* rectangles, 2½" x 7" (90 total)

42 rectangles, 2½" x 7"

From the white fabric, cut:

18 strips, 2½" x 42"; crosscut into:
  60 rectangles, 2½" x 6½"
  120 squares, 2½" x 2½"

15 strips, 2½" x 42", for borders

7 strips, 2" x 42"

From the binding fabric, cut:

8 strips, 2½" x 42"

Piecing the Blocks

1. Choose two complementary sets of three matching 2½" x 7" rectangles. Sew them together to make two units as shown. Press the seam allowances toward the darker fabric. Cut the units into two 3½"-wide segments. Repeat for all 30 matching sets of 2½" x 7" rectangles. Keep the matching segments together.

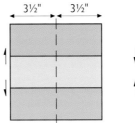 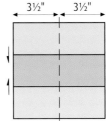

2. Sew the matching segments together as shown to make a total of 30 units.

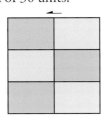

Make 30.

3. Sew white 2½" x 6½" rectangles to opposite sides of the unit from step 2. Press the seam allowances toward the block unit.

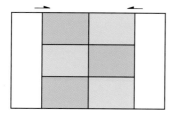

4. Draw a diagonal line from corner to corner on the *wrong* side of each white 2½" square. Place a marked square on each end of a 2½" x 10½" strip as shown, right sides together. Sew on the diagonal line. Trim away the excess fabric in the corner, making sure the triangles are sewn on correctly before you trim them. Press the seam allowances toward the darker fabric.

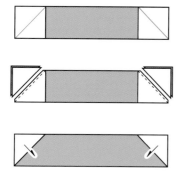

5. Sew matching strips from step 4 to the top and bottom of the block unit from step 3. Make sure the white triangles are on the outer corners. Press the seam allowances toward the strips. The block should measure 10½" square; trim if necessary. Make 30 blocks.

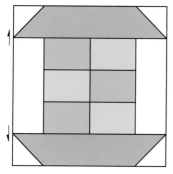

Make 30.

Block Magic!

Here's a cute alternative. If you reverse the 2½" × 10½" strips when sewing them to the block, you'll have blocks that look like spools of variegated thread!

Assembling the Quilt Top

1. Arrange the blocks in six horizontal rows of five blocks each. Sew the blocks together into rows.
2. Join the white 2"-wide sashing strips end to end using diagonal seams (shown on page 8) to make one long sashing strip. Make sure you use the strips that are 2" wide. Measure the lengths of the horizontal rows of blocks, determine the average measurement, and cut five sashing strips to this length.
3. Place the 2"-wide sashing strips between each horizontal row and sew all of the rows together. Press the seam allowances toward the blocks.

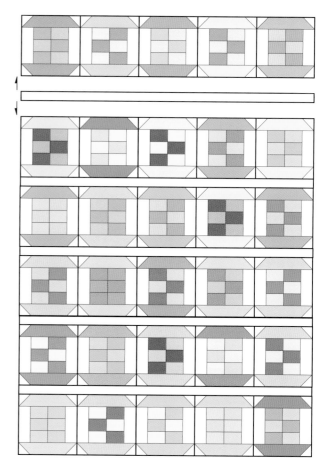

Adding the Borders

1. Join seven white 2½"-wide border strips end to end using diagonal seams. Measure the width of the quilt through the center and trim two border strips to this length. Sew the strips to the top and bottom of the quilt. Press the seam allowances toward the quilt center.

2. Measuring the length of the quilt through the center, cut two border strips to this length and sew to the sides of the quilt. Press the seam allowances toward the quilt center.

3. Join nine 2½" x 7" rectangles end to end for the pieced border. Make two for the top and bottom of the quilt. Measure the width of the quilt through the center and trim the pieced strips *equally from both ends* to fit the width of the quilt. (For example, if you need to trim off 2", trim off 1" from each end.) Sew to the top and bottom of the quilt. Press the seam allowances toward the pieced border.

Make 2.

4. Join twelve 2½" x 7" rectangles end to end. Make two for the side borders. Measure the length of the quilt through the center, including the borders just added. Trim the pieced strips *equally from both ends* to fit the length of the quilt. Sew to the sides of the quilt. Press the seam allowances toward the pieced border.

Make 2.

5. Join eight white 2½"-wide border strips end to end using diagonal seams. Measure the width of the quilt through the center and trim two border strips to this length. Sew the strips to the top and bottom of the quilt. Press the seam allowances toward the pieced border.

6. Measuring the length of the quilt through the center, cut two border strips to this length and sew to the sides of the quilt. Press the seam allowances toward the pieced border.

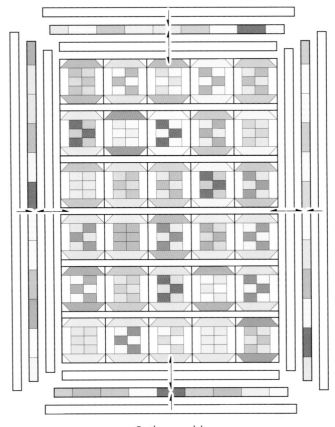

Quilt assembly

Finishing the Quilt

1. Cut and piece the backing fabric so it's 4" larger than the quilt top on all sides. Cut the batting approximately the same size.

2. Mark any quilting lines needed, then layer the backing, batting, and quilt top. Baste the layers together and quilt as desired.

3. Trim the backing and batting even with the quilt top, using your 24" quilting ruler, rotary cutter, and mat.

4. Make and attach the binding, referring to "Binding Your Quilt" on page 8 as needed.

Pieced and quilted by Sue Pfau   Finished quilt: 38" x 50"

jumping jacks

This is one of my favorite quilts. It's adorable and so easy to make. I used two charm packs, so it was extra speedy to put together. The size is perfect for a crib, making it an excellent baby shower gift. This pattern is named for my son, Jack!

Materials

Yardage is based on 42"-wide fabric, unless otherwise noted.

67 to 75 charm squares, 5" x 5", *or* 17 to 20 Layer Cake squares, 10" x 10", for blocks and pieced border

⅞ yard of white fabric for blocks, sashing, and inner border

½ yard of fabric for binding

2¾ yards of fabric for backing*

46" x 58" piece of batting

*The quilt is 38" wide. The width of a cut of fabric may be sufficient for the backing if it's 44" to 45" wide. You could get by with 1½ yards if the fabric is wide enough or if you piece using my suggestions on page 9.

Cutting

If using charm squares, there's no need to cut them. Just choose 67 of your favorites.

From the 10" squares (if using), cut:

67 squares, 5" x 5"

From the white fabric, cut:

8 strips, 1½" x 42"; crosscut 5 *of the strips* into 35 rectangles, 1½" x 5"

5 strips, 2½" x 42"; crosscut into 35 rectangles, 2½" x 5"

From the binding fabric, cut:

5 strips, 2½" x 42"

Piecing the Block Rows

1. Sew a white 2½" x 5" rectangle to a 5" square. Press the seam allowances toward the 5" square. Sew a white 1½" x 5" rectangle to the opposite side of the 5" square. Press the seam allowances toward the square. Make 35.

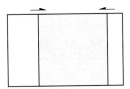

Make 35.

2. Sew seven units from step 1 together to make a row, beginning with the white 2½" x 5" rectangle on top and alternating their placement as shown. Press the seam allowances in the same direction. Make five rows, beginning each row with a white 2½" x 5" rectangle on top.

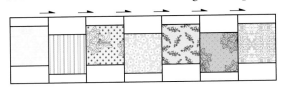

Make 5.

3. Sew seven 5" squares together end to end to make a chain of squares. Press the seam allowances in the opposite direction of the rows from step 2. Make three chains. Cut each chain lengthwise into two pieced strips, 2½" wide.

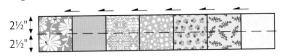

Make 3.

4. Arrange the rows and chain strips as shown in the diagram. Make sure each row starts with a white 2½" x 5" rectangle on the top of the row. After you are satisfied with their placement, check the seam allowances of the chain strips. You may need to re-press the seam allowances so they are going in the opposite direction from the seam allowances in the rows. Join the rows and chain strips, pressing the seam allowances toward the chain strips.

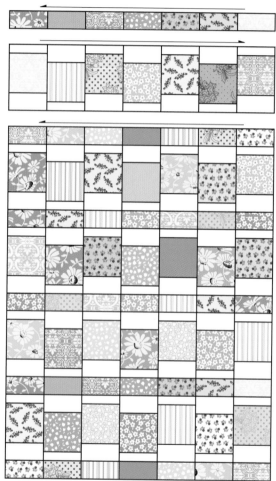

Piecing the Border

1. Sew the remaining eleven 5" squares together end to end. Press the seam allowances in the same direction. Cut lengthwise into two 2½"-wide strips. Place them next to the sides of the quilt. I rotated one so they weren't the same on each side.

2. Join three white 1½"-wide border strips end to end using diagonal seams (shown on page 8). Cut two strips to the same length as the pieced border strips.

3. Sew a white border strip to the *inside* edge of each pieced border strip.

4. Sew the border strips to the sides of the quilt with the white strips next to the center of the quilt. Press the seam allowances toward the quilt center.

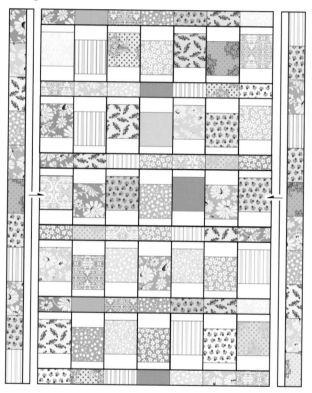

Quilt assembly

Finishing the Quilt

1. Cut and piece the backing fabric so it's 4" larger than the quilt top on all sides. Cut the batting approximately the same size.

2. Mark any quilting lines needed, then layer the backing, batting, and quilt top. Baste the layers together and quilt as desired.

3. Trim the backing and batting even with the quilt top, using your 24" quilting ruler, rotary cutter, and mat.

4. Make and attach the binding, referring to "Binding Your Quilt" on page 8 as needed.

Color Option

I couldn't resist making two of these adorable crib quilts.

"Sweet Jane" with mom Sue

I've always been interested in creating things and working with my hands. As a young adult, I tried many different handcrafts, but knitting was my favorite. When I was 32 years old and working as a flight attendant, I decided to try my hand at quilting. I started out with hand appliqué, which I was able to bring to work with me on flights. After I resigned from American Airlines in 2006, I decided to start making and selling quilts. I had a hard time finding patterns that were quick and easy, yet beautiful and interesting. I decided to try designing my own quilts, and that's what eventually led me to this point in my life.

My pattern design company is called Sweet Jane's Quilting & Design, named after my daughter, Jane, whom my husband and I adopted from China in 2006. Our son, Jack, is from Taiwan. I met my husband at work when I was a flight attendant—he's a pilot. We've been married for 10 years.

I am thrilled to be designing quilt patterns and making a living from it. People tell me all the time that I'm living the American Dream, and I agree. I am grateful, honored, and still surprised where life has led me. Thank you to all of the quilters out there who are helping me to grow my business and be successful. Happy sewing!

Visit Sue's Etsy shop at: www.etsy.com/shop/sweetjane.